What Does It Take?

Meggan A. MacKenzie

AuthorHouse™
1663 Liberty Drive
Bloomington, IN 47403
www.authorhouse.com
Phone: 1-800-839-8640

First published by AuthorHouse 01/20/2011

ISBN: 978-1-4520-9701-5 (sc)

Library of Congress Control Number: 2011900071

Printed in the United States of America

Certain stock imagery © Thinkstock.

This book is printed on acid-free paper.

authorHOUSE®

To Mom, Dad, and Brock.
Special thanks to Brian Desjarlais and Scarlet O'Neill
of Scarlet O'Neill photography
(www.scarletoneillphotography.com)

Mrs. Mary Memo was the Mayor of Cherry Town.

She wore blue dresses and big black lenses but never wore a frown.

She worked all day and worked all night, downtown at city hall,

Until she raised enough to paint a mural on the wall.

Mary walked up to the stage to start the town hall meeting.

She signalled to Art Tempera to come and join her in the greeting.

Mr. Tempera was a local artist selected for the job,

But he needed help with the big ideas or it might be a *big brown blob.*

"Hello people of Cherry Town I need your help today.

I have some ideas for the mural, but was hoping to meet halfway.

What matters to us most? What is this town all about?"

It was then that the town's ideas came freely flowing out.

MR. ED MCAPPLE:

I think education should be painted on the wall.

Without the teacher teaching there would be no town at all.

A B C's, 1 2 3's, science or Shakespeare,

Please name for me a subject that can't help in your career?!

DR. STEFFY SCOPE:

In my opinion medicine is the most important part.

Doctor's can take care of you: your teeth, your eyes, your heart.

Operations, vaccinations or perhaps some medication,

Paint that theme upon the wall. That's my recommendation!

REECE CYCLE:

Pardon me but what about all of the hard work that I do?!

I clean up the environment while cleaning up after you.

Reduce, reuse, recycle is the motto of my career.

That's my point of view and I think I made it crystal clear!

AXLE RHOADS:

Paint, food, car parts, or perhaps a pair of shoes,

I deliver these objects where they belong for you to pick and choose.

Without me driving day and night from places faraway,

How would you have the things you need each and everyday?!

No, No, No, No, you're getting it all wrong!

I help the town stay organized and keep it going strong.

Faxes, files and phone calls are all in a hard days work.

Seeing my job upon the wall would be a well earned perk!

CORI COB:

Plant, water, grow, and pick is the cycle on a farm.

My job is most important. I am the town's lucky charm.

Without a farmer in the field working dawn 'til dusk,

You would have *nothing* to eat, not even corn from its husk.

OTTO MATTIK:

The mural should represent a factory and all its shinning stars.

Factories produce a lot of things, I happen to make cars.

Check, tighten, fix, check, tighten, fix some more.

To make you what you want and need is no easy chore.

JACKIE HAMMER:

Construction should be on the wall but since you need some proof:

Fixing roads, building homes or patching up a roof.

These jobs if not completed would leave the town a total mess.

I help the town to function. I make it a success.

BILLY CLUB:

Safety is number one; correct me if I'm wrong.

I will gladly show you on a C.T.P ride along.

We watch over the community, men and women
dressed in blue.

To serve and to protect, we keep order through and
through.

Art began to feel quite nervous as he looked towards the crowd.

The town was getting rambunctious and becoming much too loud.

How was he supposed to choose from all the points of view?

He said good-bye, headed home, and hoped for a quick breakthrough.

Once Art got home he noticed there was a letter on his stoop.

He went inside and read it while he ate his bowl of soup.

It was delivered from a little girl whose name was Julia Right.

It made him feel inspired and he smiled with delight.

Mr. Art Tempera was an artist in Cherry Town.

He wore white smocks and lime green socks but never wore a frown.

He worked all day and worked all night, downtown at
city hall,

Until he was finished painting the mural on the wall.

"Ladies and gents!" Art shouted to the people at the meeting.

"I'd like to welcome you to the town hall mural revealing.

I want to thank Miss Julia Right for writing a letter to me.

Without her words I might not have seen how great our town can be!"

Dear Mr. Tempera,

    My name is Julia Right. I hope you don't mind me saying so or find me impolite. You have to stop listening to the Cherry Town adults. They all think their job is number one; that won't get you your results. Each job is so important, not one more important than the last. We're all apart of an integrated-super-all-star-cast!

    The construction worker builds a home
    While the mayor builds the town
    An artist entertains us all from sunup to sundown
    The factory worker makes the things we use
    The teacher teaches A B C's
    The secretary keeps us organized
    While the garbage man cleans up with ease
    The farmer grows the food we eat
    The trucker hauls it in
    The Doctor keeps us healthy
    While we're kept safe by policemen
Each and every single role helps to take care of me.

You see....

Not just you, or them, but WE!